BILL PICKETT
Rodeo-Ridin' Cowboy

WRITTEN BY Andrea D. Pinkney

ILLUSTRATED BY Brian Pinkney

Voyager Books
Harcourt Brace & Company
San Diego   New York   London

Text copyright © 1996 by Andrea Davis Pinkney
Illustrations copyright © 1996 by Brian Pinkney

First Voyager Books edition 1999
Voyager Books is a registered trademark of Harcourt Brace & Company.

The Library of Congress has cataloged the hardcover edition as follows:
Pinkney, Andrea Davis.
Bill Pickett: rodeo-ridin' cowboy/Andrea Davis Pinkney; illustrated by
Brian Pinkney.—1st ed.
p. cm.
Includes bibliographical references (p.).
Summary: Describes the life and accomplishments of the son of a
former slave whose unusual bulldogging style made him a rodeo star.
ISBN 0-15-200100-X
ISBN 0-15-202103-5 pb
1. Picket, Bill, ca. 1860–1932—Juvenile literature. 2. Afro-American
cowboys—Biography—Juvenile literature. 3. Rodeos—United
States—History—Juvenile literature. [1. Pickett, Bill, ca. 1860–1932.
2. Cowboys. 3. Afro-Americans—Biography.] I. Pinkney, J. Brian, ill.
II. Title.
GV1833.6P5P56 1996
636.2'0092—dc20
[B]   95-35920

FEDCBA

Printed in Singapore

The illustrations in this book were prepared as
scratchboard renderings, hand-colored with oil paint.
The display type was set in Rio Medio and Bossa Nova.
The text type was set in Stempel Garamond.
Color separations by Bright Arts, Ltd., Singapore
Printed and bound by Tien Wah Press, Singapore
This book was printed on Arctic matte paper.
Production supervision by Stan Redfern and Jane Van Gelder
Designed by Lydia D'moch

*To my mother-in-law, Gloria, and my
father-in-law, Jerry, for helping me forge
my trail*
—A. D. P.

To Eric, Jason-Eric, and Lani Wilson
—B. P.

Acknowledgments

It is with deep gratitude that the author and illustrator
wish to thank the following people and institutions
for offering their knowledge and support during the
creation of this book: Frank S. Phillips, one of Bill
Pickett's great-grandsons, who shared his family
stories about Bill Pickett's legacy; the Black American
West Museum and Heritage Center, Denver, Colorado;
the Brooklyn Public Library and branch librarian Lisa
Von Drasek; Colonel Bailey C. Hanes, Bill Pickett's
biographer; William Loren Katz, distinguished historian
and author, who has devoted much of his life to the
study of the black West; the National Cowboy Hall of
Fame and Western Heritage Center, Oklahoma City,
Oklahoma; the North Fort Worth Historical Society,
Fort Worth, Texas; and the Professional Rodeo
Cowboys Association, Colorado Springs, Colorado.

Photo, facing page: Bill Pickett at the 101 Ranch Wild West Show,
London, *circa* 1908.
Photo courtesy of Frank S. Phillips and Gilbert Pittman.

Folks been tellin' the tale
since way back when.

They been talkin' 'bout
that Pickett boy.

Growed up to be a rodeo-ridin' man.

His story keeps spreadin' on
like swollen waters in the wide Red River.

Yeah, folks been tellin' the tale
since way back when.

And they'll keep on tellin' it
till time's time ends.

—A. D. P.

Long before Bill Pickett was born, a wagon train traveled west, all the way from South Carolina. It was 1854. Eager Americans were packing up their belongings and wheeling on to the Great Plains. Some of these pioneers were white folks, looking for a new life in a new land. The rest were black—enslaved people forced to follow their masters.

The men, women, and children loaded everything they owned into those covered wagons: croaker-sacks, homespun duds, and bedclothes bundled tight. To pass the time on the slow, steady trek, the southerners sang traveling songs:

> *Westward ho, where the gettin's good.*
> *On to the land of opportunity.*
> *Westward ho, gonna stake my claim.*
> *On to Texas, the Lone Star State.*

During this long journey a baby boy was born. His name was Thomas Jefferson Pickett. He was a free-spirited young'un. But he wasn't free. Born into slavery, he had to wake when his master said *wake*, work when his master said *work*, sleep when his master said *sleep*.

On the Texas plains Thomas grew up learning to brand cattle and swing a lariat. He and his family worked for the white folks, helping them tame the parched soil into prospering feed crops.

Then the Civil War ravaged the United States. And when the war ended, all enslaved people were declared free—as free as the bluebonnet blossoms that covered the Texas prairie.

Thomas married a woman named Mary Virginia Elizabeth Gilbert. They settled with other freed slaves at Jenks-Branch, a small community just north of Austin, Texas. Heaven blessed Thomas and Mary with thirteen children.

Their second-born child was Willie M. Pickett, but folks called him Bill. A young'un who took after his father, Bill was the feistiest boy south of Abilene. He was quick as a jackrabbit, more wide-eyed than a hooty owl—and curious.

Bill's parents now owned a small plot of land, where they raised chickens and pigs and grew sweet corn, tomatoes, and collards. They sold the vegetables and fruits in town to earn their living.

Bill's brothers and sisters helped tend the crops. But Bill was always wandering off. Most days he straddled the rickety corral gate to watch cattle drives tramp along the Chisholm Trail, a gritty stretch of road that snaked from the Rio Grande to the heart of Kansas.

Bill watched as the cowboys drove thousands of ornery longhorn steers past his parents' farm to stockyards in Kansas. Each trail crew had a trail boss, a cook, and a slew of cowboys. Bill always offered them a friendly "How do?" Some cowboys tipped their hats to signal hello. But they hardly ever stopped. And behind them they left hoof-beaten dirt and the smell of adventure.

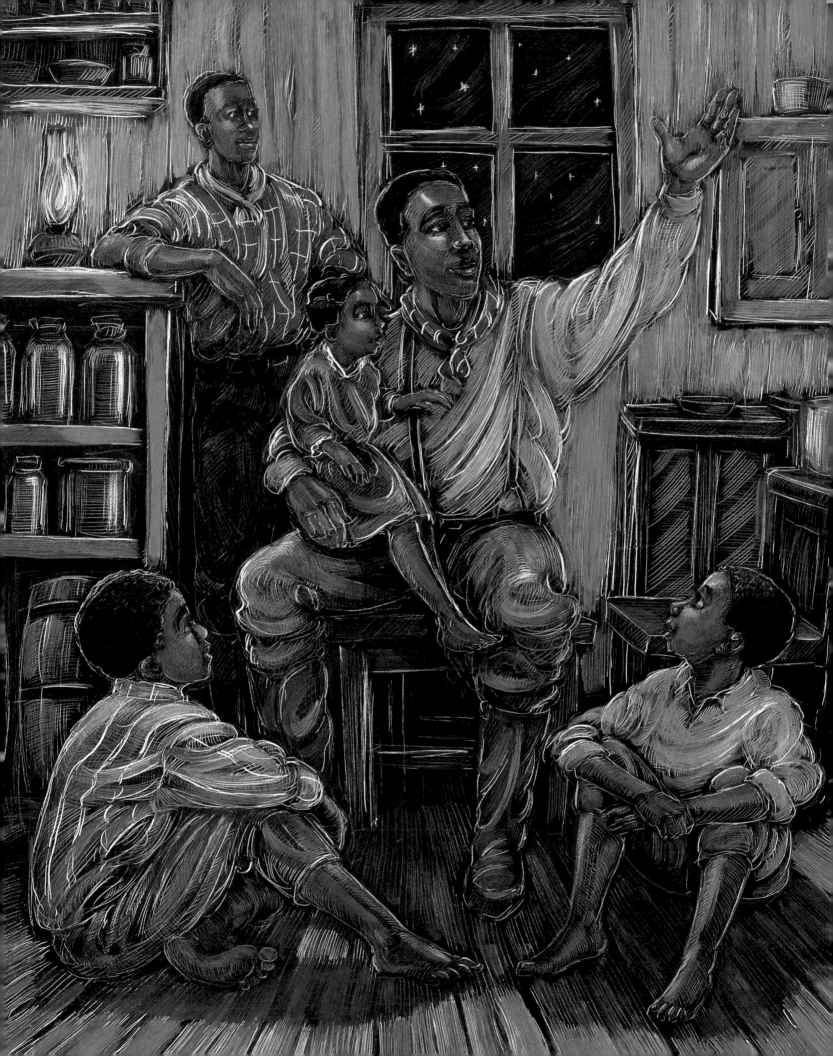

In the evenings, after the last batch of corn pone had been eaten, Bill and his family would gather round the stove fire for a night of story swapping.

Bill had two cousins, Anderson Pickett and Jerry Barton, who were trail-driving horsemen. When they came to visit, they bragged about roping steer, breaking ponies, and protecting their trail crews against buffalo stampedes. Bill and his family loved to learn their campfire songs about nights on the trail, when Anderson and Jerry slept under the black western sky with nobody watching them but the stars.

All these songs and stories sparked Bill's imagination. They made him more up-jumpy than ever. He would lie in his bed and dream of the day when he'd be old enough to rope mossback cattle and help stray dogies keep up with the herd.

One afternoon Bill was straddling the gate as usual when he
spotted an eye-popping sight. A bulldog was holding a restless
cow's lower lip with its fangs. Bill moved closer to get a good look
at how the dog's bite kept the squirming cow down. Soon Bill got
to wondering: *If a small bulldog can bite-hold a big-lipped cow,
why can't I do the same?*

Days later, on his way to school, Bill passed a band of cowboys from the Littlefield Cattle Company. The men were having a hard time branding their calves.

"Want some help?" Bill called to them. The cowboys looked at this brazen boy and went back to their work.

"I can hold one of them calves by the lip with my teeth, just like a bulldog," Bill went on. "I can do it sure as my name's Bill Pickett."

The cowboys turned out a rip-roarin' laugh.

But one of them put forth a challenge: "Let the boy go 'head and try it, if he dares."

The men roped the calf and threw it to the ground. Bill put his face down and sunk his teeth into the animal's lip. Then Bill held the calf firm while the cowboys pressed a hot branding iron into its side.

"Bulldoggin'—done by a young'un!" The cowboys cheered. Invented there and then by feisty Bill Pickett, that was bulldogging, bite-'em style.

When he was no more than fifteen and still itching for adventure, Bill set out to find his own way. Like many young'uns who came from large families, Bill had to go out and earn a living to help make ends meet.

Bill found work as a cowhand on ranches all over Texas. He spent long days saddling horses and mucking out their stalls. During the winter it was Bill's job to watch for wolves that crept up to the henhouses.

Bill learned to lasso and ride like the cowboys he'd seen pass by on the Chisholm Trail. He practiced bulldogging by catching steers that charged off into the mesquite brush. Soon Bill could tame broncs better than almost any other ranch hand. And every now and then, when work was slow, Bill went home to his mama and daddy's farm. Each time he had a new story of his own to tell his family.

Word of Bill's fearless riding spread from ranch to ranch. On Sundays folks gathered at local barnyards to watch Bill snatch a fire-eyed steer by the horns. Men, women, and young'uns rode on horseback and in their buggies to admire Bill's skill. They dropped coins in his hat to show how much they liked his horsemanship.

One morning, while he was working at a ranch in Taylor, Texas, Bill heard that the Williamson County Livestock Association had brought a fair to town. The fair included a full-scale rodeo. Men from the association had parked their wagons on a hill a few miles south of Taylor. Their rodeo was going to be a big event. Bill was determined to compete.

For the first time Bill performed his bulldogging stunt before a large rodeo crowd. As the steer thundered into the arena, Bill jumped from the back of his horse and grabbed it by its horns. Then, before the beast knew what was coming, Bill dug his teeth into the animal's tender upper lip. He raised his hands in victory as the grizzly critter went down without a fight.

Somebody let out a holler. *"Hooeee! Hooeee-hi-ooooh!"* All the folks watching the rodeo clapped and stomped.

"He throwed that beast but good!"

"That cowboy's brave clear down to his gizzards!"

"Hot-diggity-dewlap!"

After that Bill bulldogged at rodeos throughout the West. When he wasn't bulldogging for show, he still worked on ranches to make ends meet. But stories about Bill's rodeo ridin' kept on keeping on— from Texas to Arkansas to Oklahoma to Kansas to Colorado and on up through the hills of Wyoming. Now everybody wanted to see Bill perform his special bulldogging feat.

Two years later, in 1890, Bill married Maggie Turner. Bill and Maggie made Taylor, Texas, their home, and together they birthed two boys and seven girls. Sometimes Maggie and the young'uns came to watch Bill perform when he bulldogged at rodeos near their small farm. They cheered the loudest of all.

Finally Bill decided to trade ranch work for rodeo. At first it wasn't easy. He had to leave Maggie and his children for weeks at a time. And some rodeos turned Bill away. Many rodeo owners believed black cowboys should ride with their own kind.

But the newspapers didn't seem to care if Bill was black or white—Bill's *bulldogging* was news! The *Wyoming Tribune* and the *Denver Post* printed stories about the wild-riding South Texas brushpopper who could tackle a steer with his bare hands, and his bite. Slowly Bill began to earn his living as a bulldogger.

Whenever Bill came home after time on the road, he would sit his family down and let loose his tales of the rodeo. He told Maggie and their children how, everywhere he went, folks called him the Dusky Demon on account of the dusty dirt cloud that billowed behind him whenever he performed his fearless riding. All his young'uns listened close, the same way their daddy had done to his cousins' stories when he was a boy.

In 1905, when Bill was performing in the Texas Fort Worth Fat
Stock Show, he was taken by surprise. After the rodeo a fine-talkin'
man named Zack Miller approached Bill and shook his hand.

Zack Miller and his brothers, Joe and George, owned one of the
biggest ranches in the West. Their 101 Ranch spread over three
towns—White Eagle, Red Rock, and Bliss—in Oklahoma. The
Miller brothers also owned a traveling Wild West show, a spectacle
greater than the small-time rodeos where Bill usually performed.
The 101 Ranch Wild West Show had ninety cowboys and cowgirls,
three hundred animals, and sixteen acts.

The Millers' show was famous. But to make it the best, they had to
have a cowboy who could draw crowds and keep folks yip-yapping
for more. The Millers had heard about Bill Pickett. After seeing Bill
perform that day, Zack knew Bill was just the cowboy they needed.
He asked Bill to join the 101 Ranch Wild West Show. He even told
Bill that Maggie and their children would be welcome to live at the
101 Ranch while Bill traveled.

Bill didn't have to think twice. Zack's offer was the best he'd
ever got. It wasn't long before Bill and his show horse, Spradley,
became the 101's star attraction.

Soon Bill began to take his bulldogging to the far corners of the world. Crowds stood up and cheered when Bill bulldogged at Madison Square Garden in New York City.

In Mexico City townspeople filled the stands at El Toro, the national bullring, to watch the Dusky Demon face a fighting bull that was meaner than ten bulls in one.

Bill bulldogged in Canada and in South America, too. And in 1914 he performed in England for King George V and Queen Mary!

Bill's bulldog act helped turn the 101 Ranch Wild West Show into a high-falutin' wonder. Even more important, Bill helped make rodeo one of the best-loved sports of his time.

After years of bulldogging with the 101 show, Bill decided to give traveling a rest. He wanted to spend more time with Maggie and their children. So he returned to the 101 Ranch, where he lived and worked as a cowhand. To keep his skills strong, he bulldogged in rodeos closer to home.

Bulldogging lived on long after Bill died in 1932. But nobody could snatch a steer the way Bill did. When Bill's children were grown, they gathered up their own young'uns and told them about their grandfather, Bill Pickett—the feisty cowboy-child from south of Abilene who grew up to be the Dusky Demon.

More about Black Cowboys

America's history is rich with heroes. Cowboys—the men who tamed the Wild West during the late 1800s—are perhaps the most celebrated of all American legends. Nearly thirty-five thousand cowboys drove cattle when the Old West was in its prime. About one in four of these pioneers was African American.

While many enslaved black people migrated west with their masters before the Civil War, others came after the war ended in 1865 to take advantage of the work opportunities they hoped would come with their newly gained freedom. With their families these courageous people sometimes built self-sufficient, all-black towns. They became cavalrymen, trail bosses, barbers, trappers, nurses, state legislators—and cowboys.

When black men and women arrived on the western plains, they brought with them their own tradition of working with livestock and tending the land. Under the lash of slavery they had cultivated the skills of branding cattle and rounding up and taming horses. They'd worked long hours in plantation fields and had made an art of growing crops from seed to stalk under the harshest conditions.

Their knowledge—along with the care and dignity with which they performed their work—was well suited to the needs of the growing cattle business in the western states from 1865 to the turn of the century.

When the Civil War ransacked the nation, many Texans went off to fight, leaving their ranches to ruin. After the war, longhorn steers wandered wild throughout Texas, while in the northern and eastern states a demand for beef grew. During the Reconstruction period, some Texans saw a business opportunity to turn the Southwest into what came to be called the Cattle Kingdom. To make this empire grow, these businessmen needed strong, capable cowboys to work on their ranches. Black cowboys were willing and eager to take on the challenge.

In the Cattle Kingdom, skill, not skin color, was the primary concern. Along with white cowboys African Americans drove longhorn cattle for hundreds of miles to railroad cars stationed in Abilene, Kansas. Once the steers reached the Kansas railroad, they were shipped to stockyards in Chicago, Illinois, and Kansas City, Missouri.

Cowboys paid tribute to their workaday world by competing in rodeos. Rodeos began as small contests among cowboys to see who could rope and ride the best. By 1870 rodeo competitions were common and popular throughout the Southwest. They eventually became large spectator events that charged admission and paid cash prizes to participants.

Today seven standard contest events make up a rodeo: saddle bronc riding, bareback riding, bull riding, calf roping, team roping, barrel racing, and steer wrestling, which is also called bulldogging.

Bill Pickett's one-of-a-kind bulldogging established steer wrestling as a rodeo event. Today's "doggers" don't sink their teeth into a steer's lip like Bill did in his heyday. But they do try—with all the might and muscle they can muster—to wrestle the snorting beast to the dirt.

In 1971 Bill Pickett became the first African American inducted into the National Cowboy Hall of Fame and Western Heritage Center in Oklahoma City, Oklahoma. A bronze statue that depicts Bill bulldogging was unveiled in 1987 at the Fort Worth Cowtown Coliseum in Fort Worth, Texas. Today folks still praise Bill as Zack Miller, owner of the 101 Ranch, once did: "Bill Pickett was the greatest sweat-and-dirt cowhand that ever lived—bar none."

—*Andrea Davis Pinkney*

For Further Reading

Beckstead, James H. *Cowboying: A Tough Job in a Hard Land.* Salt Lake City, Utah: University of Utah Press, 1991.

Beebe, Lucius Morris, and Charles Clegg. *The American West: The Pictorial Epic of a Continent.* New York: Bonanza Books, 1955.

Blevins, Winfred. *Dictionary of the American West.* New York: Facts on File, Inc., 1993.

Brown, Dee Alexander. *Trail Driving Days.* New York: Charles Scribner's Sons, 1952.

Durham, Philip C., and Everett L. Jones. *The Negro Cowboys.* Lincoln, Nebraska: University of Nebraska Press, 1965.

Hanes, Colonel Bailey C. *Bill Pickett, Bulldogger: The Biography of a Black Cowboy.* Norman, Oklahoma: University of Oklahoma Press, 1977.

Johnson, Cecil. *Guts: Legendary Black Rodeo Cowboy Bill Pickett: A Biography.* Fort Worth, Texas: The Summit Group, 1994.

Katz, William Loren. *The Black West.* Seattle, Washington: Open Hand Publishing, Inc., 1987.

Potter, Edgar R. *Cowboy Slang.* Phoenix, Arizona: Golden West Publishers, 1986.

Seidman, Laurence Ivan. *Once in the Saddle: The Cowboy's Frontier 1866–1896.* New York: The New American Library, Inc., 1973.